FOR JADEN LEKEN KAMOIRO
AND
MEILA MAE TORONYI

RHINO
IN THE HOUSE
THE TRUE STORY OF SAVING SAMIA

DANIEL KIRK

Abrams Books for Young Readers, New York

Global map showing six of the seven continents.

The illustrations in this book were created with graphite pencil, with color added in Photoshop.

Library of Congress Cataloging-in-Publication Data

Names: Kirk, Daniel, author.
Title: Rhino in the house : the story of saving Samia / Daniel Kirk.
Description: New York : Abrams Books for Young Readers, [2017] | Audience: Ages 4–8. | Includes bibliographical references.
Identifiers: LCCN 2016020532 | ISBN 9781419723162
Subjects: LCSH: Merz, Anna, 1931–2013—Juvenile literature. | Black rhinoceros—Conservation—Kenya—Juvenile literature. | Wildlife conservation—Kenya—Juvenile literature.
Classification: LCC QL737.U63 K57 2017 | DDC 599.66/8—dc23
LC record available at https://lccn.loc.gov/2016020532

Text and illustrations copyright © 2017 Daniel Kirk

Book design by Maria T. Middleton

Published in 2017 by Abrams Books for Young Readers, an imprint of ABRAMS. All rights reserved. No portion of this book may be reproduced, stored in a retrieval system, or transmitted in any form or by any means, mechanical, electronic, photocopying, recording, or otherwise, without written permission from the publisher.

Printed and bound in China
10 9 8 7 6 5 4 3 2 1

Abrams Books for Young Readers are available at special discounts when purchased in quantity for premiums and promotions as well as fundraising or educational use. Special editions can also be created to specification. For details, contact specialsales@abramsbooks.com or the address below.

ABRAMS The Art of Books
115 West 18th Street, New York, NY 10011
abramsbooks.com

Africa, with detail of Kenya and location of Lewa Downs.

EVERYONE NEEDS A SAFE PLACE TO LIVE. Anna Merz wanted the rhinos of East Africa to have a home where they would be free from danger. There were men who wanted to cut off the rhinos' horns and then sell them to make medicine and other items. So Anna found a special place, a sanctuary on thousands of acres of rolling plains called Lewa Downs.

Anna had a big job ahead of her. She had to hire workers to build fences and roads, and guards were needed to protect the land. As the work began, she kept a close eye on the rhinos that came to live in her sanctuary.

One day Anna saw a rhino calf whose mother was not taking care of it.

The infant was weak, and clearly not well. Anna knew that without help the abandoned calf would not live. So she wrapped it in a small rug and took it home to her ranch.

Anna named her Samia. For weeks she kept the baby warm and nursed her with bottles of special formula, hoping she would survive.

And at night, to keep Samia from getting lonely, Anna brought the rhino to bed with her. She found that reading to the little animal calmed her down.

Samia soon grew strong—and noisy. She followed Anna around the ranch the way a young rhino would follow its own mother. She made funny sounds that Anna did not understand.

But Anna began to learn what Samia's sounds meant.

Eeeak?
(Where are you?)

Toot!
(I'm frustrated!)

Snort?
(What's that?)

Hoo hoo hoo!
(I'm coming!)

Anna loved Samia, but she tried not to treat her like a pet. It was important that the little rhino learn to be free and not depend on humans for her survival. Anna knew she would have to help Samia develop the skills she needed to live in the wild.

Samia liked to play with Anna's dogs, but she had to get used to the zebras, giraffes, oxpeckers, and other animals that shared her home.

Every day Anna and Samia went for long walks so the rhino could learn about her world, and discover the food that wild rhinos eat. Sometimes as Samia followed Anna, she would take Anna's fingers in her mouth . . .

. . . and as she grew bigger, Samia would often be the leader, offering her tail for Anna to hold.

Samia was a gentle creature, full of curiosity and intelligence. Still, it was not easy having a young, frisky rhino around all the time, especially since she weighed as much as a small car. Samia learned how to open gates, and she would clomp into the garden or house. She celebrated her third birthday by eating Anna's hat!

One night while Anna was in the bath, she heard the door open quietly, and then the sound *Hoo hoo hoo!*

Anna had to slip out of the tub quickly to prevent the rhino from climbing in with her.

Another time Samia sneaked into the house and became wedged in a doorway. Anna had to grease the rhino with a gallon of cooking oil so she could back out and escape!

By the time Samia was fully grown, she was spending most of her days and nights with the other rhinos on Lewa Downs. But she often returned to visit Anna, and to join her for walks in the sanctuary. Samia led the way, always ready to protect the woman who had raised her.

Sometimes they would rest together by a pond in a hidden gorge below the ranch. In the sanctuary she had created, Anna found a special friendship with Samia . . .

. . . and the love and trust between them never faltered.

AUTHOR'S NOTE

I FIRST READ ABOUT ANNA MERZ when I came across her obituary in the *New York Times*. After a long life dedicated to saving endangered African animals, Anna died in South Africa on April 4, 2013, at the age of eighty-one. I was drawn to a photo of her with a black rhinoceros called Samia. The caption explained that the rhino had followed Anna around like a dog, even after she was fully grown. As an animal lover, I found the story of Anna Merz very compelling.

I purchased a copy of Anna's book, *Rhino at the Brink of Extinction*. In it she tells how, when she was a child, her father took her to the natural history museum and showed her a stuffed dodo in a glass case. He said that the bird was extinct, because people had killed all of them, and that no matter where in the world Anna went, she would never be able to see a live one. Throughout her life Anna remembered her father's words, and she worked tirelessly to both understand and save African animals.

At the end of a career in wildlife conservation, Anna moved with her husband to Kenya, hoping for a relaxing retirement. But they soon became aware that poachers were killing rhinos for their horns and that the species was in real danger. This was Anna's call to action. She found a patron, David Craig, who owned a 45,000-acre cattle ranch. It lay on the western side of Lewa Downs, on the northern slope of Mt. Kenya. Anna convinced him that if he set aside five thousand acres, she would

ABOVE, FAR LEFT: Anna Merz and Samia. Photograph © Boyd Norton

do something to keep rhinos safe from poachers. She built fences, hired a hundred armed guards, and began bringing in rhinos from the wild for safekeeping. What had been a cattle ranch became known as the Ngare Sergoi Rhino Sanctuary.

On February 15, 1985, a black African rhinoceros named Solia gave birth to a calf. Anna realized that the mother was not caring for its baby. She took the calf back to her ranch to save it from certain death, and named it Samia. The relationship between the young rhino and the woman is at the heart of Anna's story, which has inspired animal lovers and conservationists all around the world. What Anna Merz discovered about rhino intelligence and temperament from her years working and living with Samia has changed the way people view this endangered and misunderstood species.

After learning so much about Anna and Samia, I decided to create a picture book about them. I thought that children would find the story engaging and could learn about endangered species and conservation. I began to make preliminary sketches. Despite a wealth of photographs from the Lewa Wildlife Conservancy website and images of baby rhinos I found in books, I felt I was missing something in telling the story. I decided the only way to bring more accuracy to the book was to visit Africa and see the place where Anna and Samia had lived.

In February 2016, I flew with my son, Raleigh, to

ABOVE: Photographs and a sketch by the author; Merz's house, with the author on steps; the author while on safari, photographed by his son, Raleigh. © Daniel Kirk

Nairobi, Kenya, and then to Lewa Downs. For a week we toured the now 61,000-acre conservancy. Early every morning we set out with our guide in a Land Rover to see the wild animals in their natural habitat, and I took many photographs that have helped me to bring the illustrations for this book to life. We also visited what remained of Anna Merz's house. A woman I met who had known Anna was able to explain to me how a kitchen, bathroom, and garden might have looked during the time Anna lived in the sanctuary. This journey was a once-in-a-lifetime opportunity for close encounters with African animals, and Raleigh and I learned much about the flora and fauna of eastern Africa. The experience proved invaluable in the creation of this book. I now have a much better understanding of the harsh beauty and fragility of nature, and of what we must do to protect endangered animals and their habitats.

Today, thanks to the continued support of the Craig family, the Lewa Wildlife Conservancy is flourishing. It's home to a wide variety of animals, including black and white rhinos, giraffe, ostrich, Grevy's zebras, Masai lions, African leopards, cheetah, bush elephants, and African buffalo. Twenty-five percent of the royalties from this book will be donated to the conservancy, and I encourage everyone to consider what they can do to help the endangered animals of this world. As Anna said, the rhinos' "race to extinction can be halted if only enough people care."

Visit www.lewa.org for more information.

ABOVE: Photographs and sketches by the author. © Daniel Kirk

BIBLIOGRAPHY

Books

Armstrong, Susan J., and Richard G. Botzler (eds.). *The Animal Ethics Reader*. New York: Routledge, 2003.

Merz, Anna. *Rhino at the Brink of Extinction*. London: Collins, 1991.

Other Sources

The original obituary that inspired the book, from the *New York Times* on April 21, 2013, can be found at: http://www.nytimes.com/2013/04/22/world/africa/anna-merz-protector-of-black-rhinos-dies-at-81.html

The website for the organization that keeps up Anna Merz's work is: www.lewa.org

A short video of Anna talking about rhinos and extinction can be found at: https://www.youtube.com/watch?v=P_bzbXlcjoE

A video from *Inside Edition* about saving baby rhino orphans is at: https://www.youtube.com/watch?v=cAi1wri2blw

A video that gives a good indication of what baby rhinos sound like is at: https://www.youtube.com/watch?v=LNCC6ZYI3SI